WHOSE NOSE?

by

Rebecca Phillips-Bartlett

Minneapolis, Minnesota

Credits

Images are courtesy of Shutterstock.com. With thanks to Getty Images, Thinkstock Photo, and iStockphoto. Cover – Vladimir Melnik, Viktoriia Ablohina, Michael Cola, Stephen Barnes. Recurring – Frogella, gambar_seru. 2–3 – jet 67, Frankie Gamble, Milan Zygmunt. 4–5 – Nils Jacobi. 6–7 – Gallinago_media, mostafaali123, PhotocechCZ, Aana_photo, Talented Bee. 8–9 – MehmetO, Vinnikava Viktoryia. 10–11 – Eric Isselee, Kristian Bell, Shane White, jet 67, ANNA LESKINEN. 12–13 – nis vanarin, Paul Looyen. 14–15 – Don Mammoser, Eric Isselee, Frankie Gamble, Studio 888, Natali Snailcat, StockBURIN. 16–17 – Farjana.rahman, Giedriius. 18–19 – Daria Rybakova, Iwona Fijol, Reshetnikov_art, Sbolotova, Microstocker.Pro. 20–21 – Glikiri, Reshetnikov_art. 22–23 – Agnieszka Bacal, Milan Zygmunt, Nicholas Taffs, olga_gl, Dan MacNeal, CC BY 4.0 <https://creativecommons.org/licenses/by/4.0>, via Wikimedia Commons.

Bearport Publishing Company Product Development Team

Publisher: Jen Jenson; Director of Product Development: Spencer Brinker; Managing Editor: Allison Juda; Editor: Cole Nelson; Associate Editor: Naomi Reich; Associate Editor: Tiana Tran; Art Director: Colin O'Dea; Designer: Kim Jones; Designer: Kayla Eggert; Product Development Specialist: Owen Hamlin

Library of Congress Cataloging-in-Publication Data is available at www.loc.gov or upon request from the publisher.

ISBN: 979-8-89232-737-4 (hardcover)
ISBN: 979-8-89232-787-9 (paperback)
ISBN: 979-8-89232-824-1 (ebook)

For more information, write to Bearport Publishing, 5357 Penn Avenue South, Minneapolis, MN 55419.

CONTENTS

WHOSE NOSE COULD THIS BE?

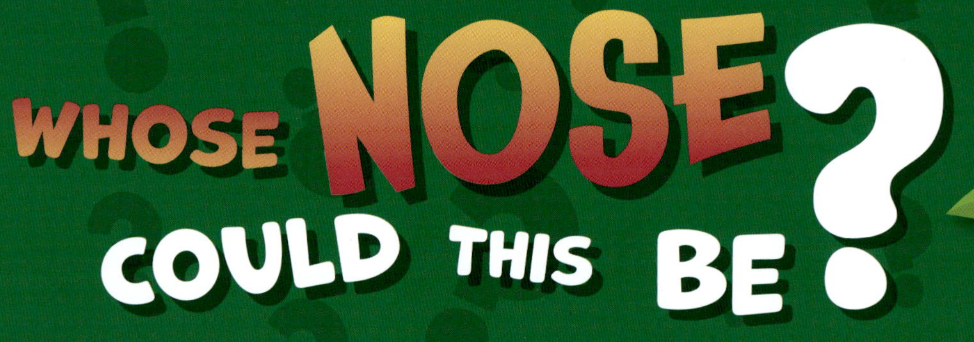

Noses help animals sniff out the world around them. But can you guess an animal just from its nose? Whose nose could this be peeking up at the sky?

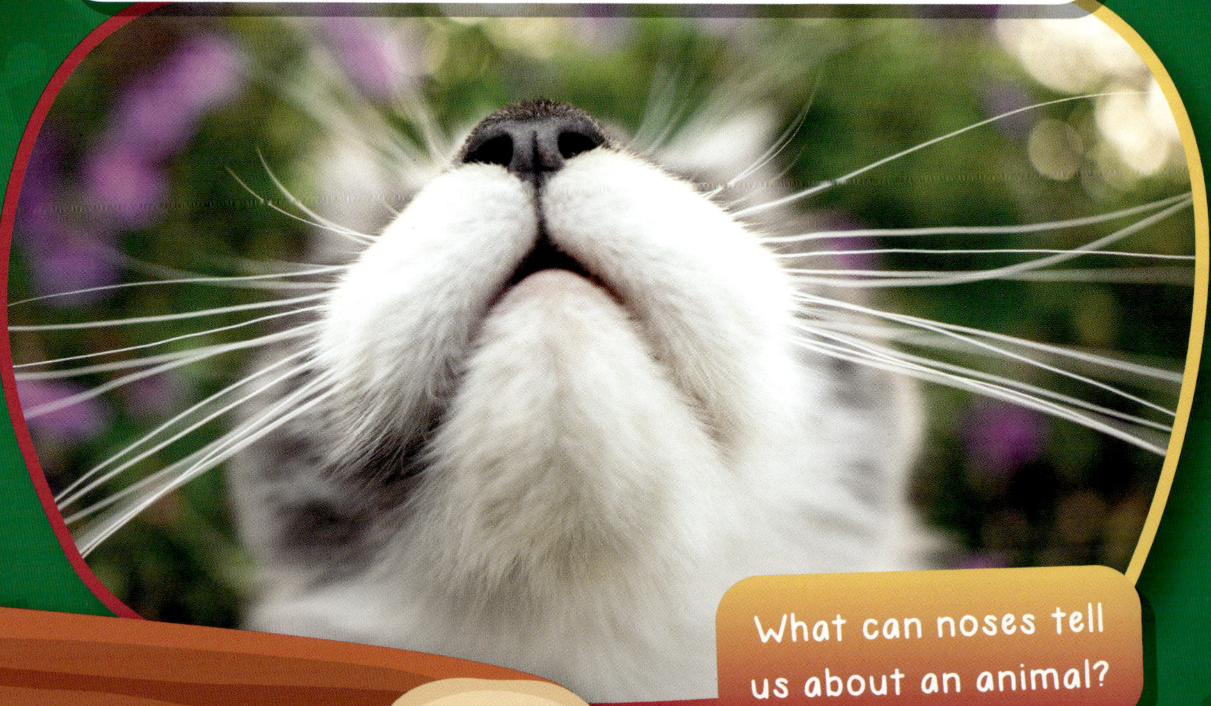

What can noses tell us about an animal?

On the following page, you will see photos of some noses and three different animals. Look at the pictures and read the clues to guess whose nose is shown. Then, turn the page to find the answer.

A CLOSING NOSE

Below is the first nose. What do you notice about it?

These **nostrils** are very flat and thin. This creature can close its nostrils. What might the animal want to keep out of its nose?

The fur around this animal's nose is a sandy color. This could help **camouflage** the creature.

Whose nose could this be? Choose which animal you think best fits the nose.

WHOSE NOSE IS IT?

It is the **CAMEL'S** nose!

Imagine getting sand up your nose!

Camels live in the dry deserts of Africa and Asia. They can close their nostrils to keep sand and dirt from flying up their noses. Camels also have long, thick eyelashes to keep their eyes safe.

A camel's nose can take in **moisture** as it breathes. This helps the animal survive when it cannot find water.

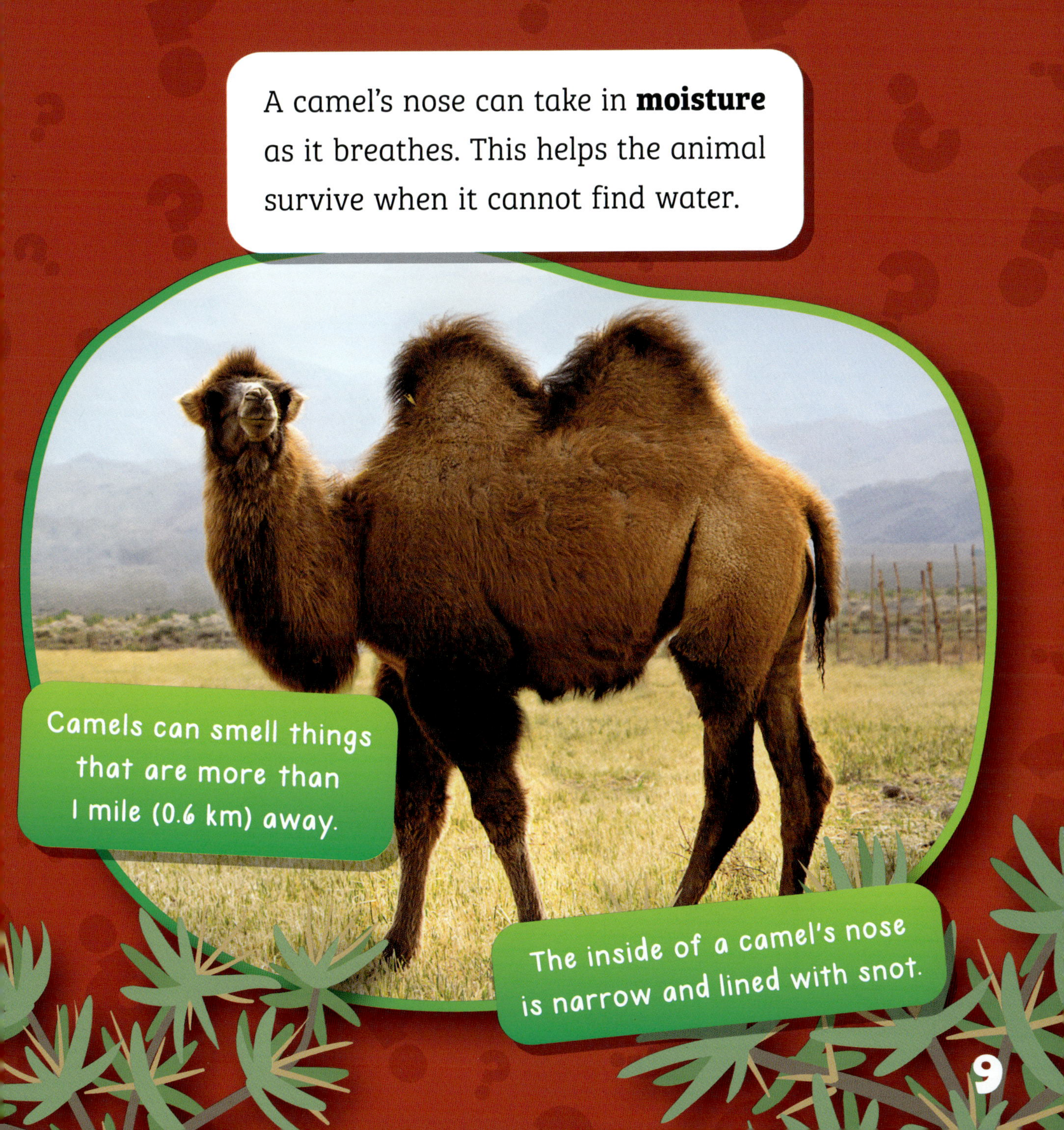

Camels can smell things that are more than 1 mile (0.6 km) away.

The inside of a camel's nose is narrow and lined with snot.

A LONG NOSE

Here is the second nose. Whose is it?

The nose is long and thin. Could it help the animal get food from hard-to-reach places?

There are two nostrils at the end of the animal's nose. Maybe they help the creature sniff out **prey**.

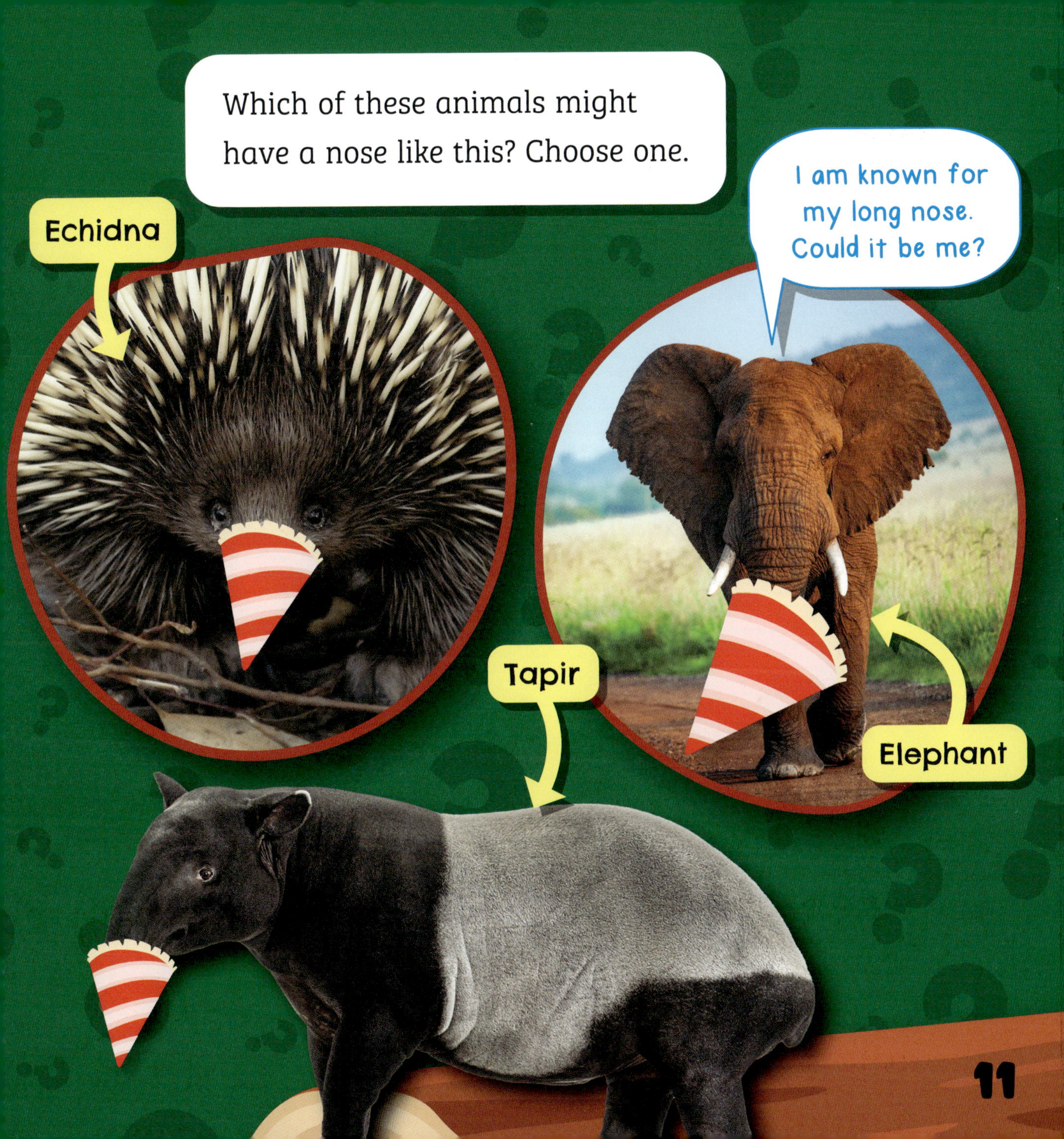
Which of these animals might have a nose like this? Choose one.
I am known for my long nose. Could it be me?
Echidna
Elephant
Tapir

WHOSE NOSE IS IT?

It is the **ECHIDNA'S** nose!

Did you know it was mine?

An echidna's mouth is on the end of its pointy nose. This spiky animal does not have teeth. Instead, an echidna uses its sticky tongue to catch and crush insects to eat.

The echidna's nose does more than just smell. It can also feel **vibrations** caused by insects crawling underground. This helps the creature find nearby prey.

A HOOK-SHAPED NOSE

The next nose is . . . wait! Is that even a nose?

Instead of a nose, this animal has a beak. Maybe it is a bird.

The beak is hook-shaped. Could this help the bird rip its prey into pieces?

What are those holes on each side of the beak?

Whose beak could this be? Here are three birds to choose from.

WHOSE NOSE IS IT?

It is the **ALBATROSS'S** beak!

Albatrosses can smell food that's 12 miles (20 km) away.

Did you get a good look at my hook?

Albatrosses are birds that spend most of their time at sea. Sometimes, food is hard to see through the choppy waves. A good sense of smell helps albatrosses find food.

Like other seabirds, albatrosses often drink salt water. But too much salt can make these birds sick. So, their noses help! They have special **glands** to remove the extra salt.

Albatross beaks have a hole on each side. The holes are called nares (NEHR-eez).

Albatrosses almost always have runny noses.

A WET NOSE

Here's another nose! Read the clues to decide whose nose it is.

The animal's nose is wet. This may help the creature have a better sense of smell.

A wet nose helps the creature's body cool down.

The nose looks bumpy.

Seal
Whose nose could it be? Make a choice from the following animals.
My nose is wet because I spend a lot of time in the water.
Dog
Bear

WHOSE NOSE IS IT?

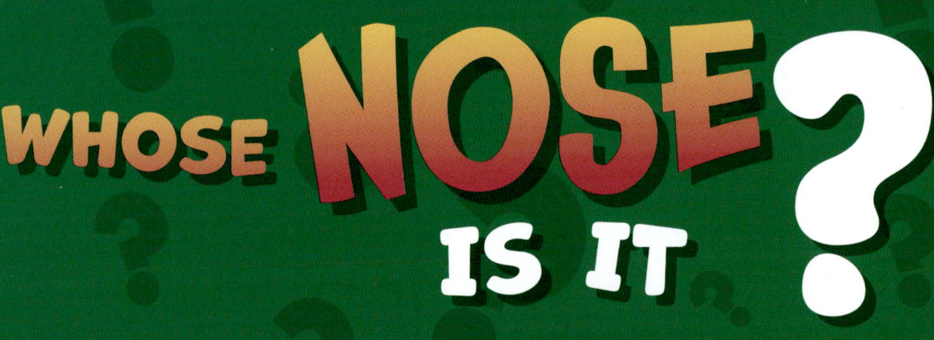

It is the **DOG'S** nose!

My nose isn't that wet . . . is it?

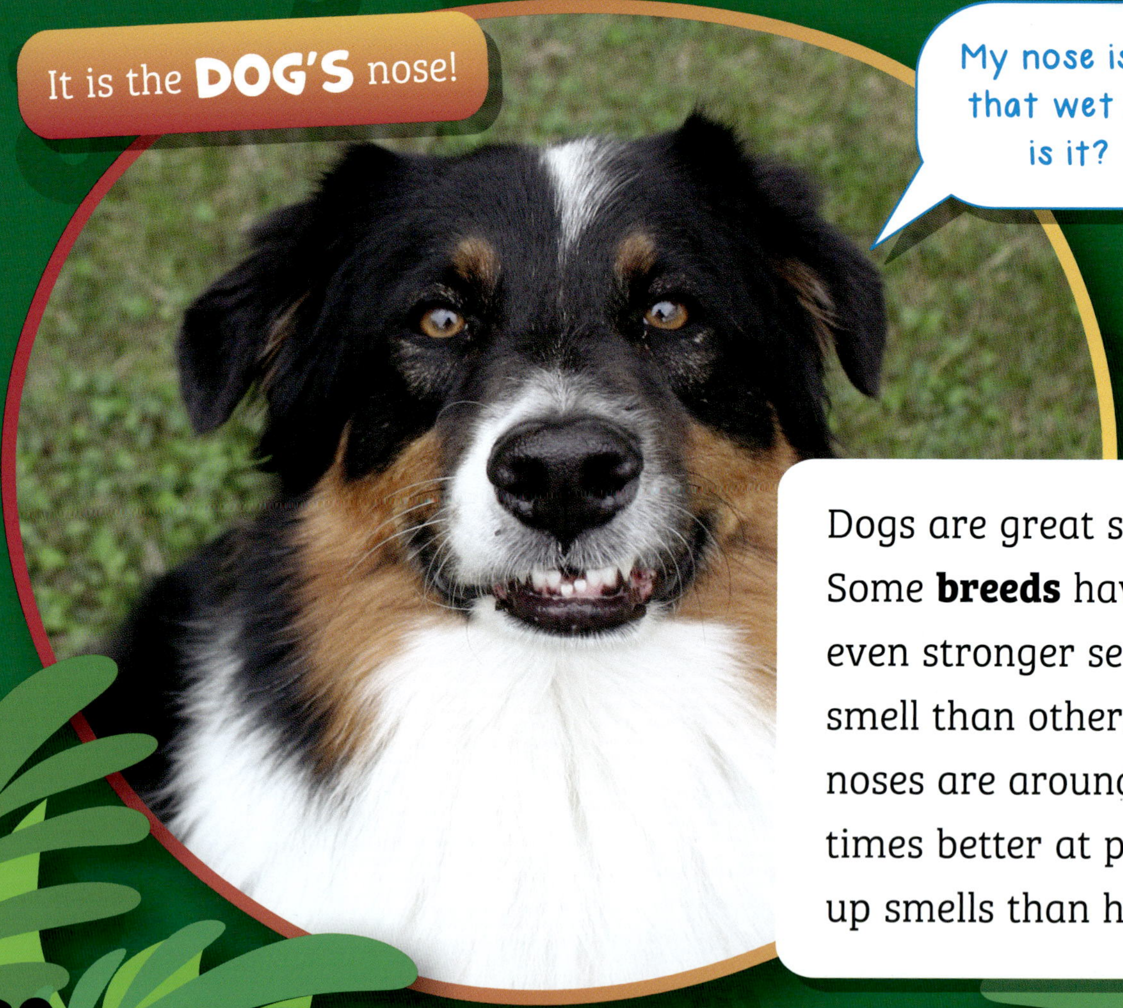

Dogs are great sniffers. Some **breeds** have an even stronger sense of smell than others. Dog noses are around 100,000 times better at picking up smells than humans.

Like human **fingerprints**, dog noseprints are different from one another. That means each doggy nose has its own pattern!

Dogs have more than 100 million **scent receptors** in their noses.

Bloodhounds have one of the best senses of smell of any dog breed.

BONUS NOSE

A STAR-SHAPED NOSE!

The star-nosed mole has an interesting nose. This mole has 22 **tentacles** around its nose. These tentacles help the mole feel the world around it.

The star-nosed mole's tentacles can touch up to 12 things each second.

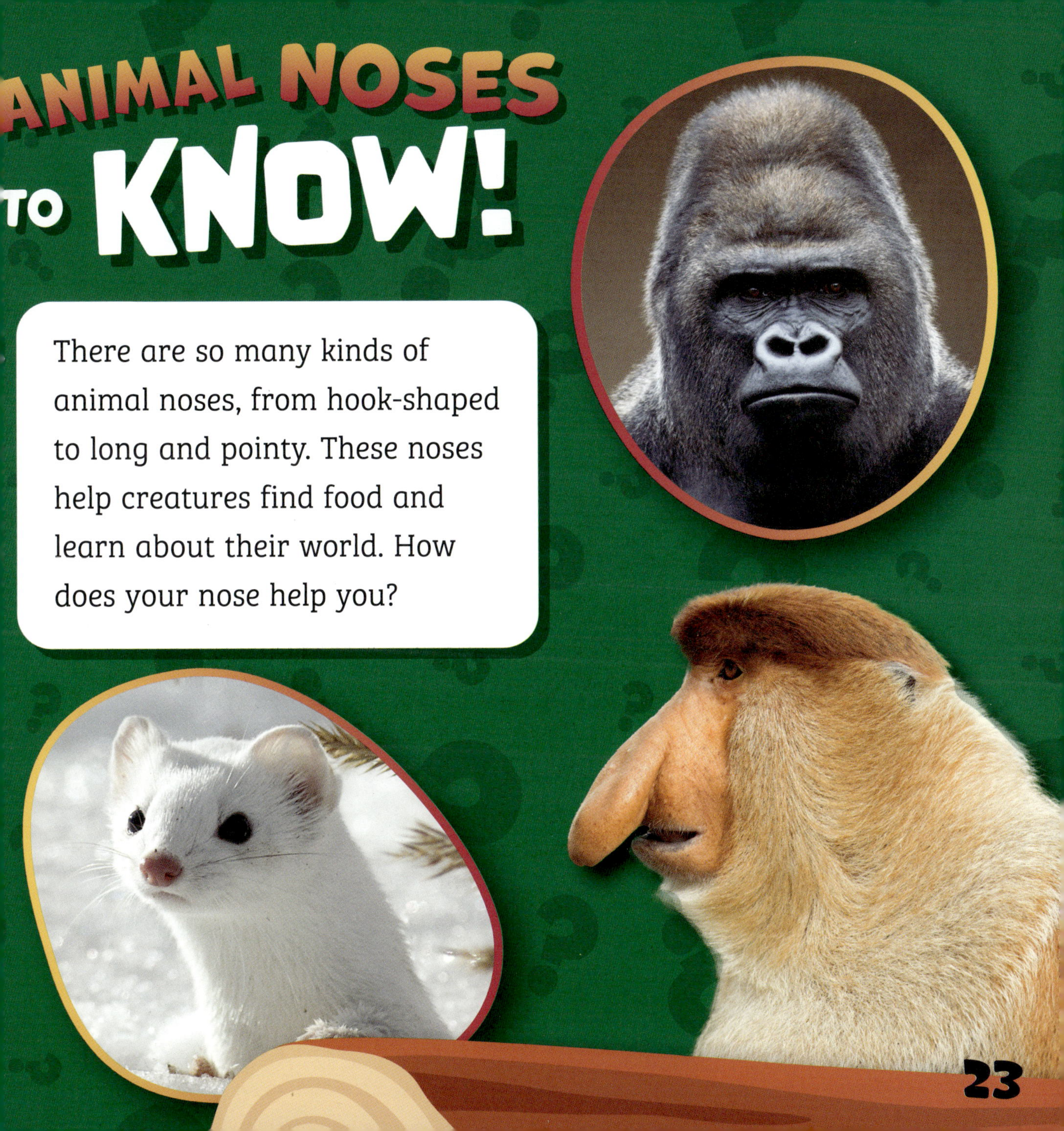

ANIMAL NOSES TO KNOW!

There are so many kinds of animal noses, from hook-shaped to long and pointy. These noses help creatures find food and learn about their world. How does your nose help you?

GLOSSARY

breeds groups of dogs that look and act in a similar way

camouflage to hide by blending into the surroundings

fingerprints marks made by pressing the tip of a finger on a surface

glands body parts that produce chemicals

moisture a small amount of liquid that makes something a little wet

nostrils two openings in the nose that are used for breathing and smelling

prey animals that are eaten by other animals

scent receptors special cells in the nose that are used for smelling

tentacles long flexible limbs on some animals used for feeling or grasping

vibrations quick back and forth shaking

INDEX